ROBERT L. PERRY

COMPUTER CRIME

A Computer-Awareness
First Book

Franklin Watts
New York | London | Toronto
Sydney | 1986

Diagram courtesy of LeeMah Security Systems, Inc.,
redrawn by Vantage Art.

Photographs courtesy of: Steelcase Inc.: p. 3;
Commodore Business Machines: p. 8;
C.H. Systems: p. 16; Texas Instruments: p. 21;
Datek Software Associates: p. 30;
The Source: p. 34; Codercard Inc.: p. 54.

Library of Congress Cataloging in Publication Data

Perry, Robert Louis, 1950-
Computer crime.

(A Computer awareness first book)
Bibliography: p.
Includes index.
Summary: Examines legal and ethical problems involving computer use, including piracy of hardware and software and the theft of information and electronic funds.
1. Computer crimes—United States—Juvenile literature. [1. Computer Crimes] I. Title. II. Series.
KF9350.Z9P47 1986   364.1'68   85-26351
ISBN 0-531-10113-4

Copyright © 1986 by Robert L. Perry
All rights reserved
Printed in the United States of America
6 5 4 3 2 1

```
j364.168 P464c
Perry, Robert Louis, 1950-
Computer crime
  $9.40
```

SOUTH

Memphis and Shelby County Public Library and Information Center

For the Residents
of
Memphis and Shelby County

CONTENTS

Chapter One
Computer Crime
1

Chapter Two
Hackers
7

Chapter Three
Hardware Theft and Piracy
19

Chapter Four
Software Piracy
25

Chapter Five
Theft of Information
and "Electronic" Money
33

Chapter Six
Computer Crime and National Security
41

Chapter Seven
You and Computer Crime
45

Chapter Eight
Computer Security in the Future
51

Glossary
58

Bibliography
61

Index
63

COMPUTER CRIME

To Jason Box,
My Favorite Young Person

CHAPTER ONE

COMPUTER CRIME

What do you think of when you hear the term "computer crime"? Do you imagine a thief sneaking into your home and stealing your personal computer? Perhaps it reminds you of newspaper stories about groups of teenagers using personal computers to break into secret government information. Or, you may think of a computer programmer who damages, destroys, or scrambles information or software stored on his or her company's mainframe computer. But would you think that a person who did any of these things is a computer criminal?

And what about the following two cases:

- Marcia used a telephone number posted on a public electronic bulletin board to gain access to information stored in a credit company's confidential files. Although this information was personal, she read it.

- Henry went to a computer users group meeting and was given free copies of dozens of programs he wanted and would have had to buy. He accepted them.

Did Marcia and Henry act wrongly? People of all ages, from teenagers to adults, have been caught, arrested, and charged with serious violations of the law in situations like these.

If you do not think what Marcia and Henry did was "criminal," you are not alone. Defining computer crime is difficult because computer crime involves many different actions. It is not as simple as a stickup or a theft. There are many "gray" areas, too. These are situations in which the courts have yet to clearly define what is legal and what is not legal.

Beyond the law, too, are many moral and ethical issues. Morality usually concerns the way any individuals in a group think they should act, while ethics are the general principles of conduct by which a group of people govern themselves. Laws are the rules, established by a governing authority, that people agree to follow. Usually they are based on a group's code of ethics. One of the main purposes of this book is to describe the various legal, moral, and ethical problems relating to computers.

WHAT IS COMPUTER CRIME?

The simplest definition of computer crime is this: the destruction, theft, or unauthorized or illegal use, modification, or copying of information, programs, services, equipment (hardware), or communications networks. It is an increasingly serious and expensive problem. Estimates of the cost of computer crime each year range from $3 billion to as much as $100 billion in theft, fraud, embezzlement, damage, hacking, and software piracy.

The money or property taken in computer crimes, however, is only the tip of the iceberg. Although most computer crimes you read about in the newspapers involve money, many others are potentially more harmful. By entering computer files or abusing confidential information, computer criminals invade the privacy of those people and companies whose information they steal or damage. Sabotaging computer files disrupts the ability of people, businesses, or even the government to do their job.

The proliferation of computers and computer terminals in businesses increases the likelihood that someone will do something illegal with the computer.

Computer crime may harm national security by making confidential military information public. If medical information on a patient stored in a hospital's computer is changed, that person could be given the wrong treatment and suffer greatly or even die.

There are five categories of computer crime:

Hardware theft and piracy. If someone steals a piece of computer equipment—for example, a disk drive, printer, or graphics tablet—that clearly is *hardware theft.* However, a more complex concept is hardware piracy: copying one computer's internal operating system and selling a second computer based on the same system. An *operating system* consists of the essential programs that act as a computer's "traffic cop," moving information and instructions around in an orderly fashion.

Software piracy. Software piracy means making unauthorized copies of programs protected by copyright. *Software* is the instructions that tell a computer what to do. Copyright is a legal system under which a person's or company's intellectual property—ideas, designs, concepts—are protected from theft. Most new books and software, songs, magazine articles, and newspapers are copyrighted. Although making copies of someone else's programs and selling them for a profit is as illegal as copying and selling a copyrighted book, the law is not very clear about making copies of copyrighted software for your own use or for gifts.

Computer hacking. Hacking is using a computer to illegally break into private computer systems or to roam through confidential, secret records. Some *hackers* (the people who do the hacking) also disrupt programs and operating systems or steal and hand out people's credit card numbers. In short, a hacker is anyone who causes havoc in computer networks.

Embezzlement and financial theft. These occur when someone uses a computer to manipulate a bank's or company's accounts and steal money. Most often, an angry, frustrated, or emotionally troubled employee does this. But frequently the thief is a professional who steals money, or a company's products, deliberately. *Embezzlement* means to steal something, usually money, you were asked to protect.

Computer fraud. Fraud differs from embezzlement in that it means to cheat or trick someone out of something they own, usually money, but it also can mean equipment, software, products, or anything else.

Espionage and sabotage. Espionage occurs when a spy, either from a foreign government or from a competing company, steals secret information. Sabotage occurs when a spy deliberately damages something so the victim cannot use it.

In computer crime, espionage usually means illegally obtaining hardware and software. Sabotage occurs if someone deliberately destroys or damages programs or equipment so the victim cannot use them without repairing or replacing them.

Information theft. This means the unauthorized or illegal copying and use of information stored on a computer system, for example, of credit card numbers. These are used to order merchandise that the credit card owner then has to pay for. A more serious threat is the duplication—by a professional—of sensitive government or company information stored on a computer system.

Now that you have some idea of the nature of computer crime and also of some of the problems involved in defining what is and what isn't a crime, we can explore these issues in more depth.

CHAPTER TWO

HACKERS

For many years, the term *hacker* defined someone who was a wizard with computers and programming. People considered it an honor to be a hacker. But when a few hackers began to use their skills to break into private computer systems and steal money and information, or disrupt the system's operations, the word acquired its current negative meaning.

Of all the kinds of computer crimes, hacking is the most likely to involve young people and teenagers. Many students may see hacking as a challenge, just as in the 1950s and 1960s it was a challenge to go drag racing and not get caught.

Some may think that discovering how to gain access to private networks and discover forbidden information is a harmless adventure. Others break into government and corporate computers because they feel that government and business are immoral. These people see themselves as "little guys" just fighting the system.

HACKING INTO NETWORKS

Hackers use a personal computer, a *modem*—a device that allows computers to "talk" over telephone lines—and a telephone to

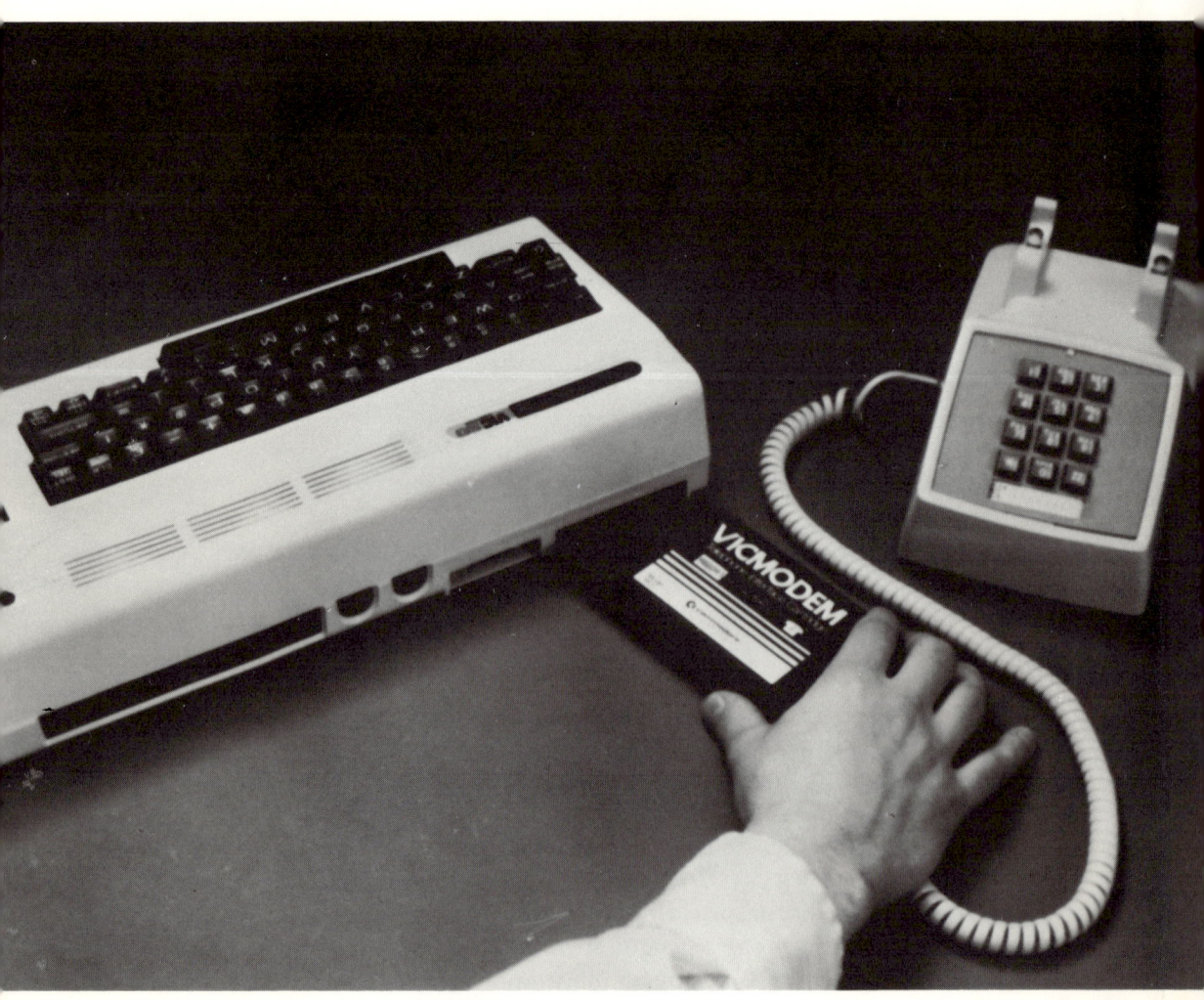

A computer-modem-telephone setup needn't be expensive. This one, combined with a video monitor and a storage device, could probably be bought for several hundred dollars.

gain access to private *computer networks*. These networks are communications systems linking computers over telephone lines.

There are dozens of private computer networks, but legal users buy the right to access each network and are given passwords and access codes. A *password* is a personal secret word that allows access to a program. An *access code* is a series of numbers and letters, often scrambled, that you must know in order to use a computer. The users also pay for the use of the information and programs supplied by the network operator.

For example, TRW Information Services has been a victim of hackers at least twice. TRW maintains computerized credit records of more than 120 million cases. It is likely that TRW has your parents' credit records on file. TRW sells copies of those records to businesses, such as department stores, that need to know whether someone has a good credit record. This is a valuable business service, and an average TRW inquiry costs about $100.

So, TRW's business depends on the privacy and accuracy of its records. Breaking into those records and stealing or damaging the credit information harms not only TRW but also the people whose records are made public or damaged. The people harmed could be your own parents and family or those of a friend or neighbor.

HACKER SLANG

What can hackers do when they break into a system? The slang hackers use to describe their actions sounds cute, but the actions are serious. Here are definitions:

Eavesdropping means to just read private information or wander around a system's software and information.

Spoofing means to pretend to be an authorized user—someone with permission to use the system—to gain improper access to a system.

Scavenging means to intercept information as it was being transferred from one system to another or was being discarded.

Diddling means to deliberately change the information stored on a network.

THE TROJAN HORSE

Hackers also can harm a system after breaking into it. A hacker can put an unauthorized program inside a system. This program, called a *Trojan Horse,* is usually used to embezzle funds. (The term comes from ancient Greek history. The Greeks sent a huge wooden horse to their enemies, the Trojans. But the gift horse was filled with soldiers, who battled the Trojans.) A Trojan Horse program may automatically transfer money from one account to an illegal account anytime a legal transaction is made.

Within a Trojan Horse program, a hacker may put a *trapdoor* program, a special program that enables the hacker to get around or damage features of the system. A *time bomb* is a trapdoor program set to go off at a predetermined time or date. These can be used to damage a system, change the contents of records, transfer information to a hidden file so the hacker can retrieve it later, embezzle money from computerized accounts, and much more.

WAR GAMES

Even "harmless" pranks can be dangerous when sensitive computer networks are involved. Although it is only fiction, the movie *War Games* demonstrated the harm pranks can do. It also showed how easy it is to break into computer networks. It showed how dangerous hacking can be, and its serious consequences. And it showed how the teenage protagonist's basic idea was morally wrong.

In real life, hacking is no more difficult to do than it was in the movie, but its results, although less spectacular, are no less serious.

In November 1983, a college science student was arrested for allegedly using his personal computer to gain access to a Defense Department computer system called ARPANET (Advanced Research Projects Agency Network), the Naval Ocean Systems Center, the Naval Research Laboratory, the Rand Corporation, and the Norwegian Telecommunications Administration. These networks stored important information about our nation's defenses and classified—or secret—research. The nineteen-year-old college student also allegedly used his home computer to obtain three airline tickets. He apparently did all of this with just a small black-and-white television set, a Commodore home computer, a modem, and a regular telephone.

During 1984, using tips learned from the movie *War Games*, four Huntsville, Alabama, teenagers used personal computers, modems, an automatic telephone dialing system, and access programs to tap into computers owned by the National Aeronautics and Space Administration (NASA). Like the nineteen-year-old student, they were caught and their computer equipment was confiscated by the Federal Bureau of Investigation (FBI). Because they were teenagers, they were not arrested. However, they were severely punished by their families and schools.

In perhaps the most famous case, a group of twelve teenagers from Milwaukee who called themselves the "414 Gang" (after their telephone area code) gained access to computers in the nuclear weapons laboratory at Los Alamos, New Mexico. Although they entered the Los Alamos computer months before *War Games* came out, these young people, aged fifteen to twenty-one, used the same techniques as the high school student in the movie. They used dial-up entry procedures and a password search. The 414 Gang also gained access to computers at Memorial Sloan-Kettering Cancer Center in New York.

HARASSMENT AND FRAUD

In one disturbing case, a group of hackers used their skills to get revenge against a *Newsweek* magazine reporter who wrote a story that criticized hackers and *phone phreaks*, who use electronic techniques to use long-distance services without paying.

In a follow-up story, the reporter said he received more than two hundred harassment phone calls. But that was the least of his troubles. A hacker broke into the reporter's confidential credit files stored by TRW Information Services. Then the hacker posted this information on electronic bulletin boards around the country. An *electronic bulletin board,* or *BBS,* is a computerized communications system on which anyone with a computer, a modem, and a telephone can swap information, place advertisements, give or ask for advice, express opinions, and send and receive electronic mail (to name some of the more popular uses).

The hacker encouraged others to illegally use the reporter's credit card numbers and generally disrupt the man's private and business life. One bulletin board even held a mock "teletrial," or electronic kangaroo court, in which obscene things were said about the writer. Some hackers even suggested that he should be killed for writing stories they did not agree with.

One thing is clear about the *Newsweek* reporter's case: the hackers who broke into TRW files violated the Credit Card Fraud Act of 1984, which became law on October 12 of that year. It provides for up to a $10,000 fine and up to fifteen years in jail for "trafficking" in illegally obtained credit card account numbers.

HACKERS AND BULLETIN BOARDS

The majority of BBSs are used by people interested in swapping information about how to use their personal computers better and enjoy them more. But bad hackers have caused police and telephone company security officers to watch bulletin boards to catch credit card fraud and to look for devices called *black boxes* that let people make long-distance telephone calls without paying.

In California in mid-August, 1984, police raided a bulletin board and confiscated the equipment. The police tried to hold the system operators (*sysops*) responsible for the messages posted on their systems, but they failed. In the California case, the system operator said he did not know illegal messages were posted on his system. The police asserted the messages were his responsibility. However, in early 1985, the case was dropped. The police could not show that the law held the sysop legally responsible for the messages on his bulletin board.

This case shows that many situations which appear to be immoral or unethical may not in fact be illegal. A law may not include the abuse of computers or computerized information in its definition of fraud or embezzlement. Or, a law may not clearly define whether computerized information is tangible property like land or a car. In general, state governments are rapidly changing their laws, and within several years these concepts should be more clearly defined.

Many BBS operators have taken steps to prevent abuses by bad hackers, mainly in the form of screening users of their boards. The sysops do not want to close off their bulletin boards, but they dislike hackers who give them a bad name and cause trouble with police officials. They know that it is their duty to make it clear that their systems are not for illegal information. They agree that they have a moral duty to prevent illegal information from being posted.

But like a newspaper that runs classified ads or a community bulletin board used for personal messages, an electronic bulletin board now cannot be held legally responsible for the *content* of the message posted on it.

NEW DEFENSES AGAINST HACKERS

Computer manufacturers also have developed new defenses against bad hackers. They defeat the most common method hackers use—automatic telephone dialing machines and programs that bypass passwords and access codes.

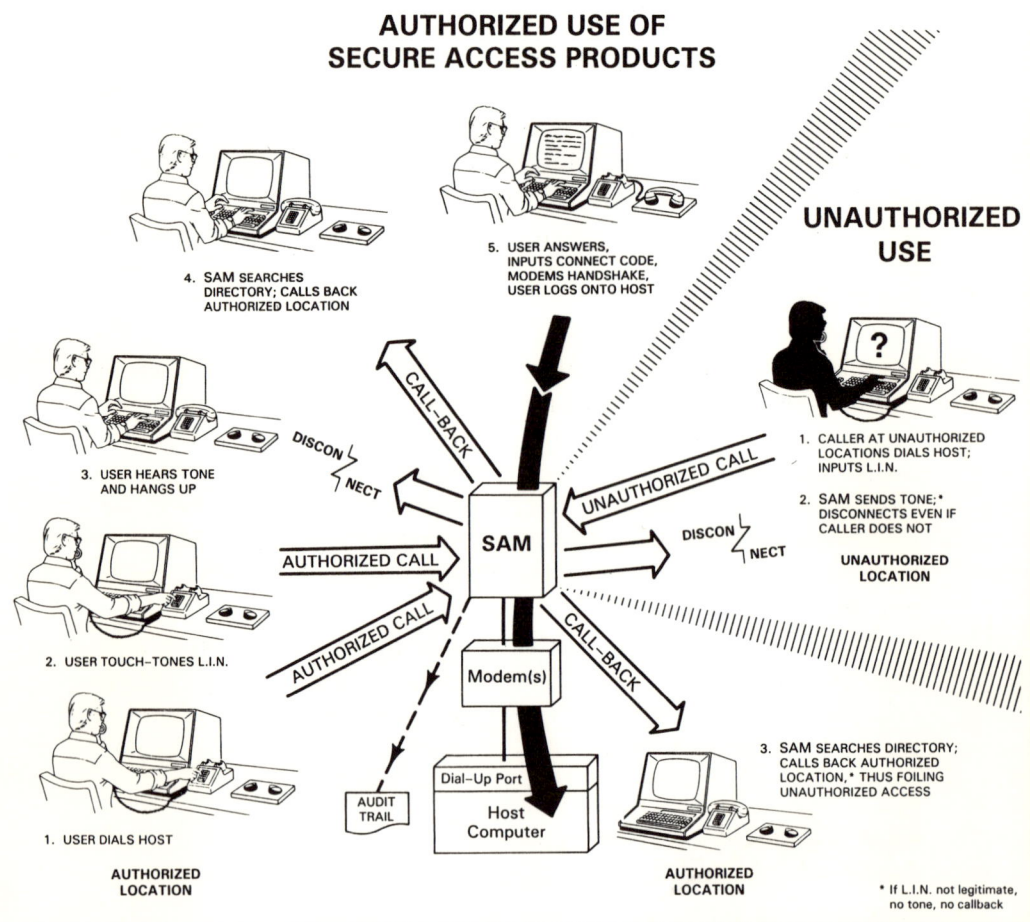

The easiest and most popular defense is a *call-back system*, a device that intercepts outside telephone calls before they reach the computer system.

The call-back device answers the call, receives the user's password and access code, and then hangs up the telephone. It then automatically calls back the telephone from which an authorized call can be made. If the call was made by a legitimate user, the computers can then "talk" to each other. If the call was made by an intruder or hacker or from any unauthorized location, the call-back device prevents the improper call from gaining access to the computer. Experts say this simple device can prevent up to 90 percent of all attempts to gain illegal entry into a computer system.

Another method is *encryption*, in which a device or program scrambles the information into a complex secret code. The military has long used encryption to protect secret information and messages.

Unfortunately, call-back devices, encryption, and other devices and techniques protect only a few computers. Most are not connected to telephone lines or communications links. Many, if not most, computer crimes are committed by people authorized to use the computers but who commit unauthorized acts while using them.

The diagram shows how SAM (Secure Access Multiport) prevents hackers and intruders from gaining access to a large computer with many terminals linked to it through computer lines. SAM is a call-back security system.

THE LEGAL AND MORAL ISSUES

Using a computer can be a good and enjoyable hobby. Learning how to communicate with bulletin boards and sending and receiving messages on them can help you make new, distant friends and teach you not only about computers, but also how to express yourself clearly in written messages.

But using a computer to get away with something illegal or of doubtful morality—in other words, hacking—should be considered in light of the trouble and harm it could cause. And hacking as a form of protest may be less effective—and is definitely less acceptable—than going through the traditional ways we have of making ourselves heard: voting, lobbying, petitioning, demonstrating, and appealing to the press.

Sleuth is a call-back security device that answers telephone calls into a computer and prevents hackers from breaking into the system.

CHAPTER THREE

HARDWARE THEFT AND PIRACY

Many of us are thrilled by tales of the sea pirates. Books such as *Treasure Island* help us imagine the glory of fighting on tall ships and taking chests filled with gold and jewels.

Today, pirates no longer hijack ships or make off with beautiful women or treasure chests. They are more likely to steal computer equipment (hardware theft) or illegally copy the design of a computer system (hardware piracy) and sell "pirated," that is, unauthorized, copies of the system. Often, this modern pirate can make more money with less risk than the pirates of old.

HARDWARE THEFT

Only ten years ago, hardware theft was not a serious problem except in the dangerous game of international espionage. Computers were large and bulky, and were difficult to steal. You had to have specialized knowledge and special equipment to run them. Computers were so expensive to buy and costly to run that businesses arranged special protection and guards to prevent theft. The risk of stealing the equipment was usually too high to make it worth a crook's while.

The microcomputer changed all of that. Today's personal computers are small, and many can be carried in a small suitcase. Portable or lap computers can be carried in a briefcase. And their peripherals—disk drives, cables, printers, etc.—are lightweight and portable. Now, it is relatively easy to steal microcomputer equipment, and theft has become a serious problem.

In response, many devices have been invented to secure computer equipment. These devices usually lock a computer or peripheral to a desk or table to prevent a thief from walking away with the equipment. One system includes a self-adhesive mat and a locking system that requires a pulling force of 6,000 pounds (2,700 kg) to remove the equipment.

The motive behind this and similar devices—or practically any security system—is to eliminate the opportunity for theft. Any police officer will tell you that most crimes occur because the opportunity is present. In short, most crimes are easy to do. Most stolen cars have keys in their ignition, for example. The same is true of computers. Most computers are not fastened to a desk. They sit there waiting for someone to carry them off.

HARDWARE PIRACY

For the most part, stealing computer hardware is a small-time crime. Far more serious is the business of stealing the design of a computer, duplicating that design, and selling the copied comput-

A computer chip is small and relatively inexpensive to manufacture, but the research and development that go into its design involve a great deal of money, labor, and creativity. Although there's a market for stolen chips, illegally copying designs is far more lucrative and a far bigger threat to the health of the computer industry.

[20]

er as one's own. The essential design of a computer system occurs at several levels: the computer chip, the internal basic input/output system (called BIOS), and the individual components of the system.

The chip, of course, is the control center of any computer and governs all aspects of a computer's operations. The BIOS is the fundamental program that links the main chip and the operating system. And the components are the hardware—the disk drives, the video monitor, the printer, the circuit boards with the wiring, and the various chips—that make up the physical parts of the system.

The designs and the ideas behind these designs are protected in two ways—by copyright and by patent. A copyright, you will remember, protects a person's rights to his or her ideas and expressions of those ideas, whether the ideas are expressed in a book or a chip design. Anyone copying the book or design without getting permission and, usually, paying a fee is in violation of the copyright law.

A new law recognizes chip designs as intellectual property for a period of ten years (books and other copyrighted materials are protected for the life of the author plus fifty years).

The BIOS and components are protected by patents. A *patent* is a legal grant which protects the rights of an inventor to his or her invention for a period of seventeen years. If an inventor did not have patent protection, anyone could take that invention and use it without paying for it. But an invention is considered to be the inventor's personal property, whose ownership is guaranteed by strict laws and a patent process. You can see patent numbers or the phrase "Patent Pending" (a patent whose number has yet to be assigned) on television sets, bicycles, stereos, and other products.

What does this have to do with computers? Many working parts and components of computers are patented too, but some companies try to duplicate the computer system and sell a similar or "compatible" computer. If they copy the patented components without permission of the patent holder, by mistake or deliberately, they are in violation of the patent law. Obtaining an original patent is difficult and time consuming and obviously requires an original invention—something not everyone can develop.

Violating chip copyrights and hardware patents is called hardware piracy. Apple Computer has successfully sued numerous Far East companies which deliberately duplicated the BIOS and components of the Apple II computer. Apple also successfully sued Franklin Computer in this country but agreed to license its technology to Franklin. Franklin pays Apple for the privilege of copying its computer system. The same principle applies to makers of IBM "clones," such as Compaq. If any of their components copy IBM components, the maker must have permission.

So, manufacturers can use a patented product or copyrighted design *if* they have the owner's written permission. Without permission, they are violating the law. Understanding copyrights and patents is not as exciting as dreaming about catching Bluebeard and his band of pirates. But the modern technological pirate works in a factory, instead of on the Spanish Main.

CHAPTER FOUR

SOFTWARE PIRACY

The essential question about software piracy is this: Is it legal to copy software and information—or not? To help you understand what is software piracy and what is not, read the following story. Then answer the questions at the end. After that, we will discuss in detail the many gray areas in the law and how the courts and software publishers are coping with software piracy.

Jason had just played *Zorgon* for the first time at his friend's house. He thought it was the best game he had ever played and wanted his own disk more than anything else. But the game cost a hefty $70, money he just did not have. And he knew his parents would not give him another advance on his allowance. After all, $70 was about six months' allowance. Christmas was six months away and his birthday almost nine, so there was no help there, Jason thought.

Just as he was bemoaning his fate, his friend Charlotte called. Charlotte said she had great news for Jason. She had just gotten a program that could be used to copy software. She asked Jason if he wanted a copy of *Zorgon*. If he did, she added, he could bring a disk to her house and she would make him a copy.

What should Jason do? The easy answer, of course, is that

Jason should run right over to Charlotte's house and get a copy. After all, it was what he wanted and he couldn't bear not to have it.

But Jason hesitated. He asked Charlotte whether it was all right to copy the program. "Isn't there a license that prevents you from giving away copies of *Zorgon*? I read the license sheet shrink-wrapped in the package."

Charlotte said that of course it was all right. "After all, doesn't your father tape movies and TV programs on his video cassette recorder? And don't you tape record albums from your stereo? And, after all, I paid for the disk, and $70 was a lot of money. So, I should be able to use the game for what I want to do with it. In fact, I'll trade you a copy of *Zorgon* for a tape of the latest U2 album. I hear it's fantastic."

What should Jason do? Should he let Charlotte give him a copy of the program? Should he trade a copy of the U2 record album for the disk? Is Charlotte's argument that she paid for the disk and can do what she wants to with it a legitimate argument? Does it make any difference that Jason's father tapes TV programs and movies on his VCR? Why would making a copy of the *Zorgon* disk be right or wrong? If Jason and Charlotte were discovered making copies of copyrighted software, would anything happen to them?

TOUGH ANSWERS TO DIFFICULT QUESTIONS

Do you think the answers to these questions are difficult? They are. Uncertainties in the law make the question of software piracy—to copy or not to copy—a tricky one.

Let's consider some of the laws that apply to Jason's dilemma: A recent U.S. Supreme Court decision in the Betamax case (which allowed the use of VCRs for at-home taping) clearly allows a person who buys a software license to make copies of that software for his or her own use. The key words here are "own use." This is the same right as that covering a person who buys a movie to watch on a VCR, or tapes a TV show to watch again. It is the same right as that of a person who buys a book or a record, and copies or tapes parts for personal use.

Does Charlotte's offer come under this "own use" law? Can Charlotte give away copies of the disk? The Betamax case shows that if Charlotte had taken *ownership* of the program, she could give away as many copies as she liked. But, as Jason correctly pointed out, Charlotte simply bought a license to use the program. Frankly, except in a few states with their own laws, whether a license gives you the right to give away copies is an unanswered question. However, many lawyers would say that giving away copies is not proper without the software owner's permission.

Much of today's problem arises from the way the software industry developed. In the past, when a software firm spent millions of dollars to write a program for a mainframe computer, it knew it would sell a handful of copies. So, it licensed each copy to protect its ownership rights and control the use of each copy. That is easy to do with only a few copies of a program. But how can they keep track of five million copies of *Space Invaders*?

In the new world of personal computers, software firms adopted the concept of "shrink-wrap licensing." Under this, the buyer agrees to be a licensee and promises not to copy the software after tearing open the plastic wrapping around the package. Several states support shrink-wrap licensing with laws, but Congress has not acted, so there are no federal laws about it. Courts have not ruled on it either, so these shrink-wrap licenses may or may not survive a lawsuit.

What about *trading*? Could Jason legally trade a tape of his U2 album for a copy of Charlotte's *Zorgon* game?

Compare trading to giving a gift. When you give a gift, you expect nothing in return. When you trade, even something as simple as baseball cards, you give something you feel is valuable and, in return, expect the other person to give you something he or she feels is valuable. Under copyright law, that makes trading a commercial transaction, and trading software is forbidden without the permission of the person or company who owns the program or game.

Making and selling unauthorized copies of software, as we have seen, clearly violates copyright law.

WHY COPYRIGHT?

If the laws are clear at least concerning certain types of copying, why do so many people break the law? Unfortunately, many people do not really understand these laws or the reasons they were created.

You already know what copyright is, but here's a new way of looking at it.

Suppose you wrote a really fantastic computer game. You gave the game away to some friends, and then a software publisher came to you and paid you $1,000 for the rights to publish the software. And you are also supposed to get a 10 percent royalty ($5 for every $50 program sold) for every copy the publisher sells. If one thousand copies are sold, you make $5,000 more; ten thousand, $50,000; and so forth.

After the software is published, you find out that Joe in the next town has made five hundred copies of your game and given them away to friends. You do some quick math and figure out that Joe has cost you $2,500. How would you feel?

Copying software is a serious problem that costs authors and software publishers billions of dollars of lost profits a year. In one situation, a Chicago software pirate was copying programs worth $50,000 and selling them, without permission, at large discounts. Another user reported receiving more than $100,000 worth of free software from members of a users group. Many of these were new programs just introduced to the market.

These losses or potential losses also reduce the incentive of some software producers to create first-rate products.

COPY PROTECTION

In response to the overwhelming wave of software piracy, many publishers try to protect their programs from being copied, using special *copy-protection programs* on the disks that prevent the main programs from being copied. These schemes can be broken, but only by sophisticated programmers. The companies using this method believe it eliminates almost all of the copying done by unsophisticated users. Again, like the companies which lock up a piece of hardware, these companies are removing the opportunity for casual piracy.

Fancy copy-protection devices also have been invented, in order to discourage more sophisticated potential pirates. One company invented a special process that etches a "fingerprint" into the surface of a floppy disk. To make a copy of the etched disk requires a master diskette. A similar approach generates an electronic signature that allows backup copies to be made but prevents copies from being made by another computer.

The most significant antipiracy effort is that of the Association of Data Processing Service Organizations (ADAPSO). Its task force has developed a software protection "fuse box" that (1) is difficult to break, (2) allows legitimate users to make copies, (3) works on a network, (4) allows users to run the software on a variety of compatible computers, and (5) works with many different programs.

COPY-PROTECTION BLUES

Despite these and other efforts, however, by the middle of 1985, it appeared that the microcomputer software industry had determined it would be difficult and almost too costly to prevent software piracy and catch and punish software pirates.

Most software companies say they will continue to include at least a basic level of copy protection with their programs, but they

**The Lock-up program protects
information from theft by scrambling the
contents on a coded floppy disk.**

plan to rely on other methods to reduce piracy and theft. Some offer inexpensive backup copies, while others plan to reduce the price of their products. All of them must rely on the understanding and honesty of their customers to prevent most unauthorized copying of software.

In business, the industry moved to a concept called site licensing. Under this, the user company negotiates the right to license and pays for the number of copies of the program it probably needs. It is then free to make these copies for that site or office. It is still not allowed to make copies to sell to other companies.

With regard to programs for large mainframe computers, software companies continue to go to great lengths to protect these expensive programs, which cost $5,000 to $250,000 or more per copy. They can and will use the law—both copyright and criminal—to protect these programs.

Companies that make computer games and inexpensive programs have pulled back from their formerly tough attitudes. Some have either settled out of court or dropped a number of lawsuits and criminal cases. They apparently began to realize how difficult and costly fighting in court could be compared with what they would gain.

The result is a strange situation: software companies cannot afford to pursue pirates in court because they do not have enough money. They do not have enough money in part because pirates have made so many copies of their programs. The ultimate loser is the consumer, who cannot get good programs and must pay a high price for those that can be bought.

HOW TO GET FREE SOFTWARE

There are many ways you can obtain copies of free software and use them without fear of violating a license agreement or copyright protections. First, any person can give away any programs they write themselves. You and your friends may write your own programs and trade them, swap them, sell them, or give them away.

Second, many users groups maintain supplies of useful free software. Third, and most important, are programs called *public domain* software. These are programs to which copyright does not apply. They were most often developed under contract to a federal agency. In general, software written for a federal agency cannot by copyrighted and can be used freely. Thousands of these programs are available from numerous sources. Your local users group or school organization should know where these sources can be found. The bibliography at the back of this book lists several references to free software.

CHAPTER FIVE

THEFT OF INFORMATION AND "ELECTRONIC" MONEY

Among the most important types of computer crimes are the theft, misuse, or damaging of information stored in computers. Sometimes money is involved, as when a computer criminal steals someone's credit card number and uses it to charge sales, or when a phony account is established into which money is transferred. Other times the intruder gains access to confidential information or steals programs.

Computer criminals can break into computer systems in many ways and often quite easily. They may:

- copy information from a storage device that is part of a personal computer system, such as a disk;

- gain access to large computers using a computer and modem;

- intercept telephone calls by tapping a telephone line or intercepting microwave transmissions;

- steal printed copies of a program or confidential information.

THE SOURCE MAIN MENU

1. NEWS AND REFERENCE RESOURCES
2. BUSINESS/FINANCIAL REPORTS
3. CATALOGUE SHOPPING
4. HOME AND LEISURE
5. EDUCATION AND CAREER
6. MAIL AND COMMUNICATIONS
7. CREATING AND COMPUTING

ENTER ITEM NUMBER OR HELP

The Source is one of the most popular data banks that can be tied into with a computer, a telephone, and a modem. Here you see the "menu," which lists broad categories of information. When you type one of the numbers, you will get an additional menu or menus that list more specific types of information or services to hook into.

These kinds of computer crimes involve some systems or technologies that need further explaining: information networks, data bases, time-sharing networks, and microwave transmissions.

An *information network* is simply an organized group of computer systems from which users in remote locations can obtain information. For example, if a computer is in New York, but a user in Chicago needs information stored on that computer, the user would call up the computer through the user's own computer or terminal and a telephone line. The computer in New York would answer the call and communicate with the user's terminal in Chicago.

A *data base* is a collection of information with a common purpose. Your record collection or collection of model airplanes could be considered a data base. In computing, a data base is a collection of information, and one gains access to an electronic data base through a computer or a terminal. There are more than three thousand on-line data bases on more than two hundred information networks. Each one charges fees for access to this information, and for use of it.

A *time-sharing network* is a group of computers whose use is granted on a pay-as-you-go basis to outside users. A company stores programs and information on its large mainframe computers. It allows outside users in different companies to buy the use of computer time, information, and programs on its own computers. Users gain access to a time-shared computer through a terminal or computer and the telephone lines.

Microwave transmissions are important in computer crime because most telephone calls are *not* carried through telephone lines or cables, but are transmitted by microwaves from one point to another. Microwaves are easy to intercept with cheap equipment. If a company or the military transmits secret information or financial transactions *without* scrambling or encrypting the transmission, a spy or white-collar criminal could intercept the transmission.

WHY INFORMATION IS VALUABLE

It may be hard at first to understand that information is expensive and valuable. Obviously, gold, silver, and jewelry are expensive and valuable. Information is valuable for the same reasons. Like gold, it is hard to find. It is difficult and expensive to process. It is difficult to keep accurate or "pure." It is in great demand. And it is useful for many purposes.

Remember the example of credit card abuse discussed in Chapter Two? In that situation, bad hackers had illegally gained access to the credit records kept by TRW Information Services. Gathering credit information about someone requires a huge network of information sources and is difficult, time-consuming, and expensive. Entering the information into TRW's computerized data bases is likewise expensive and difficult. Because thousands of businesses need quick access to that information, it is in great demand. And it must be accurate or it could harm the credit rating or personal reputation of the person on whom the record is kept. So, TRW charges a high price to allow businesses to gain access to its files.

When someone breaks into those files and takes information, he or she is cheating TRW out of all of the time, trouble, and expense it put into organizing that information. Other information can be misused and may cause harm.

Consider a personal example. Suppose you had a secret, a secret so secret you would not want anyone to find out about it. That secret, of course, is stored in a "data base" in your brain. Suppose a thief, or someone whom you knew didn't like you, was able to get inside your brain and find that secret. Then, suppose that person stood up in class and told everyone your secret. Or worse, suppose that person tried to blackmail you and force you to pay him or her *not* to make your secret public. That would, of course, be a terrible thing to happen.

Companies that store some of their confidential information in computer records have the same urgent need to protect their secrets from theft and abuse as you have to protect your secret thoughts. And, many doctors and hospitals store confidential medical records in data bases. It would be equally harmful if someone changed, damaged, or stole that medical information.

Personal information about people's work history may be stored on their employers' computers. These employees may not want anyone else to know about their medical history, their work record, or their credit record, unless they choose to tell them.

In short, every person, company, or government institution has a right to keep private, confidential information away from those who would use the information for harm. Personal and business privacy is one of our fundamental rights. Computer criminals threaten that right and can do great harm by altering or changing records, deliberately or by mistake. Or, they can cause harm by fraud, theft, or embezzlement, taking something that does not belong to them.

ELECTRONIC MONEY

Also a serious threat to business is using a computer to steal money in one of the ways defined in Chapter One: fraud, embezzlement, or theft. It may seem odd that you can steal money with a computer, but today many businesses use "electronic" money. Instead of spending stacks of dollar bills or using paper checks, banks and businesses exchange money with electronic messages called electronic funds transfers (EFT).

Say that Company A wants to send $10,000 to Company B. Often today, Company A simply sends Company B a written check, and Company B deposits it in its bank account. Using "electronic" money, Company A sends a message to its bank to take $10,000 out of its account and send it electronically to the account kept by Company B at a different bank. A's bank sends an electronic check to B's bank and reduces the balance in Company A's account by $10,000. B's bank receives the electronic money and adds it to B's account. No actual money or even a check changes hands, but Company B now has the $10,000 sent to it by Company A.

A criminal uses a computer to take money in numerous ways, but all of them involve taking money electronically from one bank account without the owner's permission. A common way criminals do this is to use phony accounts. A criminal sets up a phony bank account and then puts a Trojan horse program into a company's computer. The computer puts money into the criminal's phony bank account whenever the Trojan horse program instructs it to do so.

Another way to steal electronic money is to set up a program to intercept messages and change the name of the person or company to whom the money is being sent.

During the past twenty years, many complex schemes have been discovered to steal electronic money. Today, almost all banks and businesses use sophisticated ways to code their electronic money messages so they cannot be stolen, but no codes are perfect and criminals work hard to find ways to break these coding schemes.

THE LAWS

Congress and the state governments have begun to crack down on white-collar computer criminals. Congress passed a law in 1984 that, for the first time, makes it a federal crime to take anything of value by unauthorized use of a computer. This could be anything from stocks and bonds to merchandise, and includes credit card fraud and abuse, and other information theft. The same law makes it illegal to gain $5,000 during a year or cause $5,000 or more in damage from such illegal access. It also makes it illegal to obtain information now protected by federal laws. And it makes it illegal to gain access to any federal computer or obtain defense information without permission. Penalties include up to a year in jail and fines up to $5,000 or twice the value of the stolen service or damage.

In addition, more than twenty-five states have laws that prevent the use and abuse of computers for theft or fraud, and most of the other twenty-five states are considering similar laws. State, local, and federal law enforcement agencies (the FBI, in particular) are working to train their agents in catching computer criminals.

To deal with the possible threat to privacy created by the collection of information on individuals by business and the government, Congress and the state governments are now studying what types of information should be allowed in data bases as well as how to protect the information once it is stored on computers. In the future, it may be that less-personal information will be stored in computers, and that information will be better protected from intruders.

CHAPTER SIX

COMPUTER CRIME AND NATIONAL SECURITY

Although it is wrong for hackers to break into secret government computers, most do not deliberately mean to harm the United States or endanger our security. Of course, their actions cause a lot of trouble and disruption. They may affect military, space, and defense agencies, which have to reprogram their computers and install improved security procedures and devices.

But others *do* intend to find military secrets. For example, a student enrolled at Carnegie-Mellon University during 1982 used a computer in his dormitory room to gain access to the U.S. Department of Defense network. He then moved into the Air Force computer system. His actions were discovered, and when he was questioned about what he meant to do, he said he was gathering "missile plans" to publish in an underground newsletter. He accessed directories and read files as he was "browsing around for something interesting."

An expert noted at the time that anyone who gets into the national defense computer network can gain practically unlimited access to any of the computers belonging to the universities or corporations linked to the network. As the Milwaukee 414 group's actions showed, even casual browsers can innocently destroy records or change operating systems. When anyone does find interesting information, stealing it becomes tempting.

SERIOUS QUESTIONS ABOUT SECURITY

Most disturbing, however, is this question: if amateurs are able to get so far before they are caught, how far do professional computer spies get? What secrets do they steal without ever getting caught? Although the answer has never been discussed by the Defense Department, serious breaches of security have probably happened before and will happen again.

Another serious problem is the theft of computer hardware and software and its sale or transport to countries that the U.S. government forbids to have it.

In mid-1984, the director of the Central Intelligence Agency (CIA) said in a speech that some three hundred companies operating in thirty countries were trying to send essential computer equipment and high-technology products to communist countries. The director added that many similar firms may have gone undetected. He emphasized that computer and electronic firms in the well-known Silicon Valley region of California were the primary targets for these espionage efforts. He said that obtaining sophisticated computer technology was the "single most significant industrial technology acquired by the Soviets since the end of World War II."

ESPIONAGE BY FOREIGN GOVERNMENTS

During the 1970s alone, the CIA believes the Soviets obtained six important technologies related to microcomputers, including how to prepare, make, test, and assemble computer chips. Without U.S. technology, the Soviets would have been unable to develop many of their current weapons. In fact, the U.S. government publishes a list of more than two hundred computer-related products U.S. companies are not supposed to supply to the Soviet Union or its allies.

Several large shipments of computers were stopped in 1984. But a lot of U.S. technology, which we sell or give to our allies, is bought or stolen from them by countries that are not supposed to get it.

Foreign governments, and not just the Soviet Union, also try to intercept or eavesdrop on the telephone and computer communications of both the U.S. government and U.S. companies doing business in those countries. In New York and Washington, for example, the Soviet's residential compounds and office buildings bristle with sophisticated antennas. Off the U.S. coast, numerous Soviet trawlers, also laden with sophisticated communications equipment, eavesdrop on practically every telephone call made in this country.

Of course, the National Security Agency, the CIA, and other U.S. intelligence agencies are supposed to be eavesdropping on the Russians as well. Foreign governments and foreign companies that learn military or commercial secrets could use them to leap ahead of us in making weapons. They could figure out how to defeat our defenses and could sell their goods and products in the commercial marketplace.

PROTECTING COMPUTER COMMUNICATIONS

Computer security experts and the government do take many steps to protect telephone and computer communications. All secret or confidential communications or computer transmissions are encrypted, or scrambled, with codes almost impossible to decipher or break. The Defense Department has a program to protect its computers from intruders and another to develop an even more advanced computer.

Basically, the military divides the memory capacity of a computer into different secrecy levels or classifications from unclassified to most sensitive. To gain access to each secure level requires new types of permission, new passwords and access codes, and many more steps. These methods and tight management of the weakest link in the chain—the human link—help make military computers secure.

The most secure available method to protect computer communications through microwave or satellite is encryption—the scrambling of the information or programs using a sophisticated code and key. Experts advise businesses with overseas branches to encode, or encrypt, all of their confidential information, such as financial information, marketing plans, trade secrets, passwords, customer lists, and company strategies. However, even the most complex encryption systems are not immune to decoding.

It is easy to see how the interception of secret military and government information can endanger national security. For example, reportedly the main reason the British won the Battle of the Falklands was that U.S. spy satellites intercepted Argentina's encoded communications. U.S. experts broke the code and gave it to the British, who then knew practically every move the Argentinians were going to make before they made it. A similar event occurred during World War II, but on a much larger scale. The British broke the German High Command codes with the Enigma machine (an early computer) and consistently knew or could figure out German plans.

Today, the enormous volume of computer-to-computer communications is growing each year. They all must be thoroughly protected.

If all of this sounds like a bad James Bond novel, remember that it is all too real. Computer espionage years ago replaced the cloak and dagger game. The secure country today is the one with the most secure computers and communications networks, not the one with the most tanks and artillery.

CHAPTER SEVEN

YOU AND COMPUTER CRIME

In earlier chapters, we saw a few ways you could be affected by computer crime. Most likely, if you or your friends own a personal computer, you may want to or be asked to make copies of a copyrighted program. Or perhaps, you will join a bulletin board and find access numbers, codes, and passwords for a credit reporting data bank posted among the messages. How you act in these and many other situations will be up to you, but when you do act, try to be guided by these three considerations: ethics, morality, and legality.

Although these already have been defined, each will now be defined again since many people confuse them.

Ethics and morality are almost the same. Ethics are the general principles of conduct by which a group of people govern themselves, and are developed by that group of people over a period of time. Morality is the way any individual in that group thinks he or she should act. Often, a person's morals are stricter than the ethics of the group. Sometimes, they are less strict. Legality refers only to the laws made by the people; these laws are often based on their code of ethics, however.

Laws must be passed by a legislature or established by a court decision. Laws dictate rules for human behavior, and spell out punishment for breaking those rules. But laws alone cannot dictate all human behavior. Ethics and morality, and social customs, conventions, and habits, also affect it.

Computer crime—hardware and software piracy, hacking, information theft, etc.—by definition violates the law. But as noted in several chapters, even the law is unclear about many issues. When the law is unclear, people may follow their morals or ethical rules of conduct.

PUTTING YOURSELF INTO THE PICTURE

Described below are a number of situations in which you may find yourself. After each situation, several questions are posed about how to act. It is up to you to determine how you should act. You be the judge of your own actions and those of your peers.

- In the movie *War Games*, the main character tried to get into his school's data base to change his girlfriend's biology grade from an F to a B. In the movie *Oxford Blues*, a desperate student paid a computer hacker $1,000 to break into a college's rating system and move his name from a low position on a list of students to the second position, so he would be accepted at Oxford University in the United Kingdom. Did both of these students commit crimes? If you think they did, why? If not, were they morally justified in their actions? Was one or the other justified? Why?
- In another situation, John and Martha were the best computer programmers in their high school. A police detective contacted them and asked them to help gather information about a company suspected of smuggling drugs. The detective asked the pair of computerists to break into the company's computer system through the telephone and copy financial information and other pertinent facts stored there. But the detective asked them not to

tell anyone about their activities because it was dangerous and because no search warrant or court order allowing a wiretap had been obtained.

Martha thought they should help the detective because the cause was good. She reasoned they were not going to change, damage, or destroy the information. In fact, the whole idea was to get into and out of the system without being detected. Surely the detective knew that what she asked them to do was all right. Or, if not, the detective would protect them if they got into trouble.

Unlike Martha, John was hesitant and worried. He said he thought the tap was probably illegal and all three of them could get into serious trouble if they did it. They only had the word of the detective that the company *might* be linked to drug smuggling.

Should John and Martha help the police detective? What legal and moral issues are involved? What could happen if they did violate the law and were caught? Would they be right if the information they copied helped the detective arrest and convict company officials of drug smuggling? Would they be right, or wrong, if it didn't?

■ In a third situation, Robin had just added a communications modem to her computer system. She dialed the number of a local bulletin board and hooked up to it. As she was browsing through the messages, she saw a message that gave a list of telephone numbers and another list of what seemed to be access codes and passwords. The message hinted that the lists would tie a hacker into an important computer network, but did not say so directly.

Should Robin immediately notify the telephone company of the message? Should she explore further and call the number and use the codes and password to find out if they did indeed let her break into an important network? If Robin calls the telephone company and reports the message, should she also warn the sysop that she is going to call? Should she post another message on the system warning other users that the message has been reported?

Would you consider Robin to be a "fink" or a "stooge" if she reported the message? What should Robin do if she calls the sysop first and the sysop tells her to mind her own business? Is Robin legally or only morally obligated to notify the police, or to notify anyone at all, or should she just ignore it and not get involved?

- In another case, Clarence loved to play a video arcade game called *Sky Blast Plus*. Clarence also liked to program his personal computer, and he decided to program a game similar to *Sky Blast Plus*. He worked hard on the program, and it turned out to look and play an awful lot like *Sky Blast Plus*. He showed the program, *Space Killers*, to his friends and they loved it. Soon, he was giving copies away right and left, and within a week, a local software house, Lazy Day Software, offered him money if he sold them the rights to his game.

Just a day before he signed the contract, he was contacted by a representative for the company that makes *Sky Blast Plus*. The representative told Clarence that the company had reviewed a copy of *Space Killers* and warned Clarence that it violated copyright laws.

Clarence was upset. He said, "Okay, I borrowed the idea from *Sky Blast Plus*, but I didn't *copy* the program. I used a different computer with different chips, and I added a lot of features *Sky Blast Plus* doesn't have."

Should Clarence sign the contract with Lazy Day Software? Did the representative of *Sky Blast Plus* act properly?

- Deborah, too, found herself in a dilemma because of her knowledge of computers. Her father, a doctor, had purchased a computer to store his patient records. Deborah had done well in computer classes at school, and her father asked her to help him set up the system. As she was setting up patient records and entering information, she stumbled upon some startling information. The mayor of her city, who was a patient of her father's, had an incurable disease. Yet, the mayor was running for reelection, claiming to be "fit as a fiddle and tight as a drum."

Deborah knew that the mayor was misleading the public for his own private and political reasons. If reelected, he could resign and name his successor. Deborah also knew that medical records were confidential, but she was not a doctor, nor was she technically her father's employee.

Should Deborah let it be known to other people that the mayor was not in good health, but in fact, was more than likely going to die within months after the election? Should she stay silent? Should she tell her father what she found out and ask him to persuade the mayor to make it public? Does she have an obligation to the public as a private citizen? If she discloses the mayor's medical records, can her father get into trouble? What kind of trouble would it be—a violation of the law or a violation of medical ethics?

THE PENALTIES

These moral, ethical, and legal dilemmas are fictitious, but similar things happen in real life every day.

What could happen to someone caught violating the new federal anticomputer crime law or one of the state laws (see Chapter Five)? A person under eighteen would be turned over to the local juvenile court and the case handled in private. A person over eighteen (sixteen in some states) would be treated as an adult. Depending on the seriousness of the violation, the charge could be a misdemeanor or a felony. A felony is the more serious charge.

So far, some people under the age of twenty-one have been prosecuted for breaking into computer networks. Others have not been prosecuted for several reasons, but an important one is that the government and the companies involved would have to reveal their computer security measures in open court. They do not think it wise to make their precautions public and, by doing that, show everyone how to take advantage of them.

In some cases, the young people involved were sufficiently frightened by having the FBI confiscate their equipment that they quickly agreed not to do it anymore. Several young people have actually started helping the government and private business protect their computers from outside intruders.

Other reasons business and government may not prosecute computer criminals include these:

- Companies are reluctant to press charges and be embarrassed in public.
- They prefer to prosecute adults and not young people.
- It is difficult to detect certain types of computer crime as well as find out who committed them.

If you are involved with computers, you should realize that you can do much good and much harm with a computer. Before you use a computer to communicate with a network, make copies of software, or seek out an adventure on a bulletin board, think about your actions. Ask yourself whether you truly believe what you are doing is right or wrong, good or bad. Consider the possible results—will it harm someone else, could it violate a law, could it damage someone else's property? Consider the possible consequences—both positive and negative—before you act. In this way, you can enjoy your computer to the fullest and avoid your own moral, ethical, or legal dilemma.

CHAPTER EIGHT

COMPUTER SECURITY IN THE FUTURE

VOICE RECOGNITION

If you have ever seen *Star Wars* or a *Star Trek* rerun on television, you already know the future of computer security. In fact, some of the ways the spaceship *Enterprise* protected access to its computer are already being used today. To enter the most secret data banks on the *Enterprise,* Captain Kirk has to speak to the computer with a specific code sequence. Only when the computer recognizes the sequence and Kirk's voice patterns does it allow him access to the data bank.

This process is called *voice recognition.* Today, in many top-secret military installations, a similar security system is already in place. In the future, preventing access to information with a talking and—more impressively—a hearing computer will be as common as passwords are today.

In voice recognition, you speak into a microphone. A microprocessor between the microphone and the main computer's memory turns the voice into digital signals the computer can understand. The computer matches the signals against signal patterns stored in its memory. If the two match, the computer responds that the match has been made and it allows access to the system. Explaining it takes much longer than it takes to happen. Even with today's primitive voice recognition systems, the computer can translate the voice patterns and respond in less than one second.

The main problem holding back the technology today is memory capacity. A lot of computer memory is required for a computer to understand just one spoken word. Soon, however, even the average home computer will have significantly more memory than it does today. More sophisticated personal computers will have much more, and the quality of voice recognition will improve. The talking and hearing computer *Star Trek* predicted may become reality.

FINGERPRINT SCANNERS

A hearing computer is only one of many exotic means already used on a small scale to protect computers from illegal access. Several devices read fingerprints and can verify your identity. To use a *fingerprint scanner*, you put your finger on a pad, and a small camera inside the device makes an electronic record of your fingerprint pattern. Of course, everyone knows that each person has his or her own unique fingerprint. The police have used fingerprints for identification for decades.

The computerized fingerprint scanner stores all of the patterns in its memory and, within seconds, compares your pattern with those in its memory. If the patterns match, the device lets you have access to the computer. Fingerprint identification devices are already used to prevent unauthorized access to sensitive rooms within buildings. For example, a large bank would use a fingerprint device to protect the rooms where the cash was counted. A military installation would use it to protect a secret communications operation.

In the future, banks may attach fingerprint devices to their automated teller machines. But first they must deal with the issue of privacy. Some people strongly oppose giving their fingerprints to a bank because they believe it is an invasion of privacy.

EYEBALL SCANNERS

Even more exotic than fingerprint scanners are *eyeball scanners.* For many years, it has been known that the pattern of the eye retina—the part of your eye that receives images and sends them to the brain's optic nerve—is more unique than a fingerprint. So, several companies have developed devices that scan the retina and compare it to retina patterns stored in a computer. If the retina pattern of the person looking into the scanner matches a stored pattern, then the computer allows access.

This type of scanning, too, requires large amounts of computer memory. Today, a minicomputer or part of a large mainframe is used for this process.

BIOMETRIC DEVICES

Eye retina scanners, fingerprint scanners, and similar machines are called *biometric* security devices. They are all relatively new technologies. In the future, they will be refined and improved so they can be used with a personal computer. But many people object to them because they invade one's privacy and they are annoying. Sticking a finger into a machine or looking into a box that looks like an overgrown pair of binoculars makes people uneasy. So it is likely that these biometric machines will be used only to protect the most sensitive computers and rooms.

SMART CARDS

More likely to become popular in protecting access to computers is a new device that looks like a credit card but which contains a tiny computer chip—the *smart card.* Smart cards are versatile and

[53]

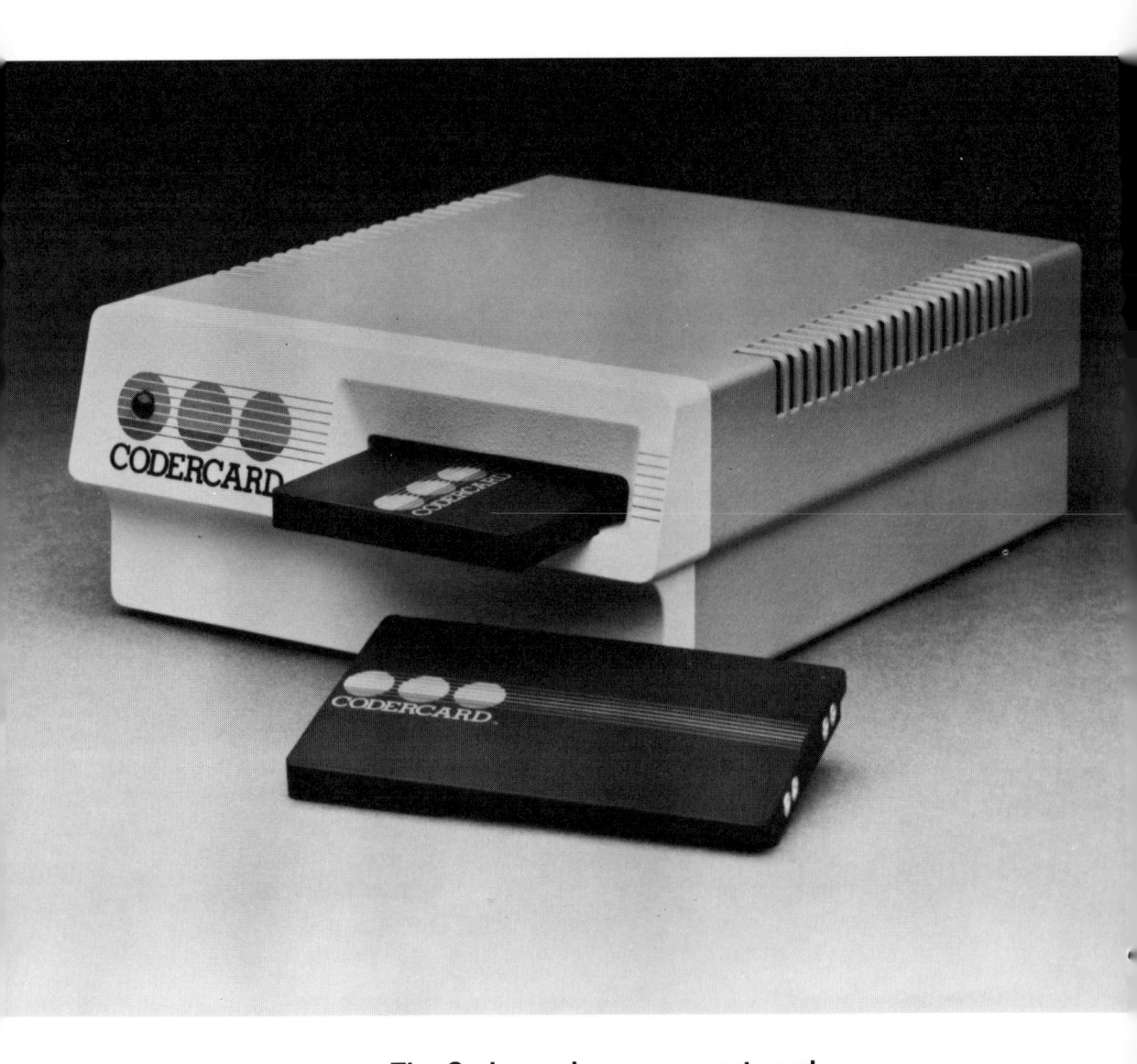

**The Codercard uses a smart card
—a credit-card-sized microprocessor—
to protect computers from theft and misuse.**

can be used not only for computer security, but also as a medical information bank, as a personal information bank, or for practically any purpose that requires a lot of information to be carried in a small space.

For example, the U.S. military may replace the traditional dog tag with a smart card that has a member of the armed forces' entire personal history and military record on it. In France, where the smart card was invented, one experiment has put a family's medical history on a smart card. When anyone in the family visits a doctor, the doctor puts the smart card into a card reader and the history is flashed on a video monitor.

For computer security purposes, the smart card can be used to verify all users and keep track of all attempts to access the computer. One company has developed the first secure smart card. This card is slightly thicker than a credit card. It stores a unique identification number that no one can tamper with or change, and includes a chip that can generate billions of unique security codes.

To use the card, you slip it into a card-reader attached to or built into a computer terminal or personal computer linked to a network or large computer. The smart card sends its ID number and a new, unique password to the main computer. Inside the main computer's memory, a smart-card monitor system checks the ID number, manipulates its password generator, and sends a new password back to the smart card. The smart card in the personal computer must duplicate the password generation and reach the same result before access to the computer is granted.

The secure smart card can be modified to work with a biometric security system, like the eyeball scanner, or more traditional checks such as the PIN (personal identification number) now used with bank teller machines.

With the serious growth in credit card fraud, it is likely that banks and credit card companies will be the first to use the smart card to replace plastic credit cards. Banks will also use them to replace access cards for their automated teller machines. And business and government will use them to improve their current security methods.

In the future—within the next ten years—electronic banking at home through personal computers will probably become popular. But one of the important drawbacks to home banking is that people fear thieves will abuse their electronic checking accounts. This fear is reasonable, although experts say that electronic checking is safer, on average, than using a regular paper checkbook. Passwords, ID numbers, and access codes will not be enough to protect your accounts, so banks are testing smart cards as the best solution to home banking security.

In the future, people may carry around a purse or wallet full of smart cards the way people today carry around a pocketful of credit cards.

BUILT-IN COMPUTER SECURITY

As these new personal ways to prevent computer crime become possible, highly technical ways to build security *into* computers are also being developed. New programming methods make operating systems secure from intrusion. New computer chips with built-in encryption make scrambling software and information inexpensive and easy. New plug-in modules for personal computers also allow software and information to be scrambled. New types of floppy disks scramble information when it is stored on a disk. And new lockout devices prevent a computer (a TV, a VCR, a stereo, or any other electronic device) from working unless you know the right code.

SECURITY AND YOU

The search for the perfectly secure computer will go on. For every new security method, there exists a way to defeat it. New, stricter laws, providing for tougher fines and longer jail terms, may be passed. But many people, lured by the prospect of stealing and not getting caught, will continue to steal, defraud, and embezzle money and information. Misled hackers, believing falsely they are modern Robin Hoods or driven by a feeling of rebellion, will keep trying to break into confidential data bases. And many people and businesses will be harmed by their illegal actions.

Whether computer crime will worsen during the future cannot be known. What is known is that computers and information networks of the future will make up an ever greater part of our lives. But computers are just tools; they are not good or bad. How you use them—what you do with them—leads to good or bad, right or wrong, legal or illegal results. The choice is up to you.

GLOSSARY

Access code—A special code used to gain entry to a computer system or software.

BBS—See *Electronic bulletin board.*

Biometric security device—A device that works in conjunction with a computer to identify computer users by fingerprints, palm prints, eyeball patterns, and other biological features.

Black box—A device that allows a person to make long-distance telephone calls without paying for them.

Call-back system—A device placed between a modem and a computer to prevent illegal break-ins by hackers.

Computer network—Any collection of computers and terminals which communicate through telephone lines.

Copy-protection program—Software that prevents a user from making a copy of a program or information.

Copyright—A legal system protecting a person's intellectual property—ideas, designs, concepts—from theft.

Data base—A collection of files, records, or information with a common purpose, for example, library file cards.

Diddling—When a hacker deliberately damages, alters, or destroys information on a computer network.

Eavesdropping—Hackers' slang for looking into someone else's computer files without permission.

Electronic bulletin board (BBS)—An electronic message system that users access through a central computer.

Embezzlement—The act of illegally taking something that you were asked to protect.

Encryption—A sophisticated technique that scrambles information or programs with a coding scheme.

Ethics—The general principles of conduct by which a group of people govern themselves.

Eyeball scanner—A computer security device that measures the unique patterns within the retina of the eye. Before it grants access, it compares the patterns of people seeking access to a secure area to retina patterns of those allowed access.

Fingerprint scanner—A computer security device that lets only users with recognizable fingerprints use a system.

Fraud—To cheat or trick someone out of something he or she owns.

Hacker—Originally, a computer wizard or someone adept at programming. Now, anyone who misuses a computer to illegally access private computer networks.

Hardware piracy—Stealing the operating system of a computer in order to build a similar or identical computer.

Hardware Theft—Stealing a piece of computer equipment.

Information network—Also called data base service, data base network, or information service, it is any private computer network that stores data bases and sells access to them to the public.

Laws—The rules, established by a governing authority, which a group of people agree to follow. Usually, laws are based on a group's code of ethics.

Modem—A device that allows computers to communicate through telephone lines.

Morality—The way any individual in a group thinks he or she should act.

Operating system—Governs how the components of a computer and its programs work together in harmony.
Password—The secret word a person uses to access restricted computer programs or information.
Patent—A legal grant that protects the rights of an inventor to his or her invention for seventeen years.
Phone phreaks—People who use illegal methods to make long-distance telephone calls.
Public domain—Programs not protected by copyright and thus available to any user free of charge.
Scavenging—Hackers' slang for intercepting information a legal or authorized user is discarding.
Smart card—A new type of microprocessor on a chip embedded in a plastic shell.
Software piracy—The unauthorized copying of programs protected by copyright.
Spoofing—Hackers' slang for pretending to be an authorized user to gain access to a private network.
Sysop—Slang term for a bulletin board system operator.
Time bomb—A type of Trojan horse program that works only at certain times or dates. See *Trojan horse program.*
Trapdoor program—A type of Trojan horse program that lets the intruder interfere with the normal workings of a computer system. See *Trojan horse program.*
Trojan horse program—A program routine secretly hidden inside another program and most often used to embezzle money or disrupt a computer's operations.
Voice recognition—An electronic process by which a computer recognizes the spoken human voice.

BIBLIOGRAPHY

Asimov, Isaac, et al. *Computer Crimes and Capers.* Chicago: Academy Chicago, 1983.

Bitter, Gary L. *Computers in Today's World.* New York: Wiley, 1983.

Bove, Tony; Cheryl Rhodes; and Kelly Smith. *Free Software.* New York: Baen Books, 1985.

Cooper, Carolyn E. *Electronic Bulletin Boards.* Watts, 1985.

Froelich, Robert. *Free Software Catalog and Directory.* New York: Crown Publishers, 1984.

Gader, Bertram, and Manuel V. Nodar. *Free Software for the IBM PC.* New York: Warner Books, 1984.

Glossbrenner, Alfred. *How to Get Free Software.* New York: St. Martin's Press, 1984.

Heller, Dave and Dorothy. *Free Software for Your Apple.* New York: Enrichment Press Free Software Series, 1984.

_____. *Free Software for Your Atari.* New York: Enrichment Press Free Software Series, 1984.

_____. *Free Software for Your Commodore.* New York: Enrichment Press Free Software Series, 1984.

_____. *Free Software for Your TI*. New York: Enrichment Press Free Software Series, 1984.

Hintz, Sandy and Martin. *Computers in Our World, Today and Tomorrow*. New York: Franklin Watts, 1983.

International Resource Development. *Computer Security—Hardware, Software, Systems and Facilities Markets*. Norwalk, CT: Report #623, October, 1984.

Landreth, Bill. *Out of the Inner Circle, A Hacker's Guide to Computer Security*. Bellevue, WA: Microsoft Press, 1985.

Levy, Steven. *Hackers*. New York: Doubleday Anchor, 1984.

Lewis, Sasha. *Plugging In: The Microcomputerist's Guide to Telecommunications*. New York: Chilton Publishing, 1984.

Lyons, Norman R. *Understanding Computer Crime*. New York: Alfred Publishing, 1984.

Myers, Lory L. *How to Create Your Own Computer Bulletin Board*. Blue Ridge Summit, PA: Tab Books, 1983.

Owen, Jan. *Understanding Computer Information Networks*. New York: Alfred Publishing, 1984.

Perry, Robert L. *Owning Your Home Computer, The Complete Illustrated Guide*. New York: Dodd, Mead, 1984.

Schabeck, Timothy A., Ph.D. *Managing Microcomputer Security*. Plymouth, MI: Computer Protection Systems, Inc., 1983.

INDEX

Access code, 9, 58
Air Force, 41
Apple Computer, 23
ARPANET, 10–11
Association of Data Processing Service Organizations (ADAPSO), 29

Bank accounts, phony, 38
Banking, electronic, 56
Basic input/output system, 22
BBS, 12–13, 58
Betamax case, 26
Biometric security devices, 53, 58
BIOS, 22
Black boxes, 12, 58
Built-in computer security, 56
Bulletin board, electronic, 12–13, 59

Call-back system, 15, 58
Categories of computer crime, 4–5
Checking accounts, electronic, 56
Chips, computer, 21, 22
CIA (Central Intelligence Agency), 42, 43

Circuit boards, 22
Code, access, 9, 58
Codercard, 54
Coding schemes, 38
Compaq, 23
Components, 22
Computer chip, 21, 22
Computer crime, defining, 2
Computer fraud, 5
Computer hacking, 4
Computer networks, 9, 58
Congress, 38
Copy protection system, 29, 31, 58
Copyright, 4, 22, 58
  why do it, 28
Costs, 8
Credit Card Fraud Act, 12

Data base, 35, 58
Defense Department, 10, 41, 42, 43
Defenses against hackers, 13, 15
Diddling, 10, 58
Disk drives, 22

[63]

Eavesdropping, 9, 59
Electronic banking, 56
Electronic bulletin boards (BBS), 12–13, 59
Electronic checking accounts, 56
Electronic fund transfers (EFT), 37
Electronic money, 37–38
Embezzlement, 4–5, 10, 59
Encryption, 15, 44, 56, 59
Enigma machine, 44
Espionage, 5
    by foreign governments, 42–43
Ethical issues, 2
Ethics, 45, 59
Eyeball scanners, 53, 59

Falklands War, 44
FBI (Federal Bureau of Investigation), 11, 39
Felony, 49
Financial theft, 4–5
"Fingerprint" device, 29
Fingerprint scanners, 52–53, 59
Foreign government espionage, 42–43
414 Gang, 11, 41
Franklin Computer, 23
Fraud, 5, 12, 59
Free software, 31–32
Fund transfers, electronic, 37
Funds, embezzling, 10
"Fuse box," 29
Future security, 51–57

Games, copying, 25–26

Hackers, 7–17, 59
Hacker slang, 9–10
Hacking, 4
    into networks, 7, 9

Hardware, 22
    piracy, 4, 59
    theft, 4, 19–20, 59
Hearing computer, 51

IBM clones, 23
Information,
    theft of, 5, 33–37
    value of, 36–37
Information network, 35, 59

Laws, 38–39, 46, 49–50, 59
Legal issues, 17
Legality, 45
Licensing
    shrink-wrap, 27
    site, 31
Lock-up program, 30
Long-distance phone calls, 11

Medical information bank, 55
Memorial Sloan-Kettering Cancer Center, 11
Memory capacity, 52
Menu, 34
Microcomputer, 20
Microwave transmission, 35
Modem, 7, 8, 59
Money, electronic, 37–38
Moral issues, 2, 17
Morality, 45, 59

NASA, 11
National security, 4, 41–44
National Security Agency, 43
Naval Ocean Systems Center, 11
Naval Research Laboratory, 11
Networks,
    computer, 9, 58
    information, 35, 59
    time-sharing, 35

Newsweek magazine, 11
Norwegian Telecommunications Administration, 11

Operating system, 4, 60
"Own use" law, 26–27

Password, 9, 60
Patents, 22, 60
Penalties for computer crime, 49–50
Phone phreaks, 11, 60
Phony bank account, 38
PIN (personal ID number), 55
Piracy
    hardware, 4, 21–23, 59
    software, 4, 25–32, 60
Pirated copies, 19
Printer, 22
Privacy, 36–37, 39
Protecting computer communications, 43–44
Public domain software, 32, 60

Rand Corporation, 11

Sabotage, 5
SAM (Secure Access Multiport), 14
Scanners
    eyeball, 53, 59
    fingerprint, 52–53, 59
Scavenging, 9, 60
Scrambling of information, 44
Security
    biometric, 53, 58
    built in, 56
    future, 51–57

Security and you, 56–57
Security breaches, 42
Security, national, 4, 41–44
Shrink-wrap licensing, 27
Silicon Valley, 42
Site licensing, 31
Sleuth, 16
Smart cards, 53–56, 60
Software, 4
    free, 31–32
    piracy, 4, 25–32, 60
Source, 34
Soviet Union, 42–43
Spoofing, 9, 60
Sysops, 12–13, 60

Theft
    financial, 4–5
    hardware, 4, 19–20, 59
    information, 5, 33–37
Time bomb program, 10, 60
Time-sharing network, 35
Trading software, 27–28
"Trafficking" of credit card account numbers, 12
Trapdoor program, 10, 60
Trojan Horse program, 10, 38, 60
TRW Information Services, 9, 12

VCR home taping, 26–27
Video monitor, 22
Voice recognition, 51, 60

War Games, 10–11
World War II, 44

You in the picture, 46–49

[65]

ABOUT THE AUTHOR

Robert Perry is a computer consultant and the author of numerous special reports, hundreds of magazine articles, and the book *Owning Your Home Computer*. He also has been an editor at a number of publications, including *Boys Life, Personal Computers Magazine,* and *Mechanix Illustrated.* Mr. Perry lives in Florida. *Computer Crime* is his first book for Franklin Watts.